Ages
4-5

Smart Sk
Preschool
Basic Skills

Carson Dellosa Education
Greensboro, North Carolina

DISNEY **LEARNING**

Published by
Carson Dellosa Education
PO Box 35665
Greensboro, NC 27425 USA

Printed in the USA • All rights reserved.   ISBN 978-1-4838-6140-1
01-053217784

Contents

What Is Your Name?

This is Mickey.
Mickey is his name.
Print your name.

Preschool Basic Skills © Disney CD-705390

Draw a picture of yourself.

Animal Connections

These birds are hungry! Draw lines connecting each bird to a tasty bug.

Draw lines to match each animal with the correct drawing.

Follow the Path

Draw lines to make a path for the mice around the cherries.

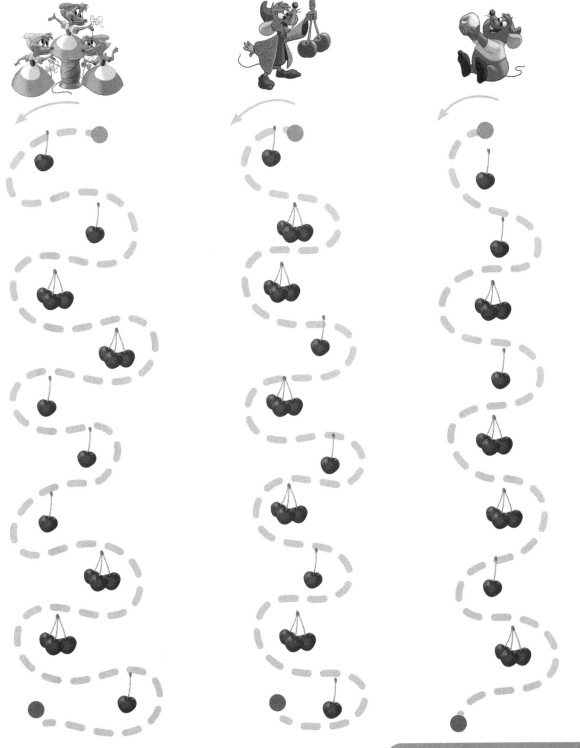

Trace the lines around the objects.

Pluto Needs Your Help

Follow the arrows.
Trace the lines.
Help Pluto find his toys.

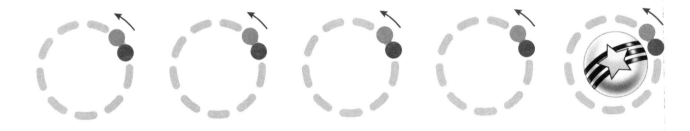

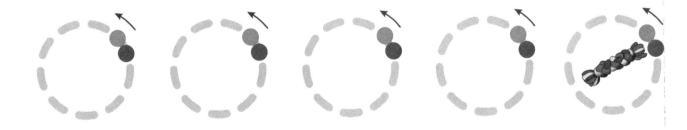

Help Figaro find his toys.

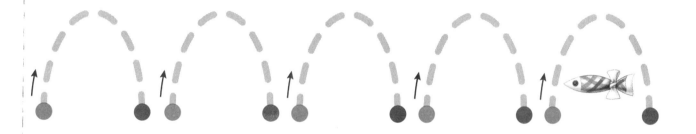

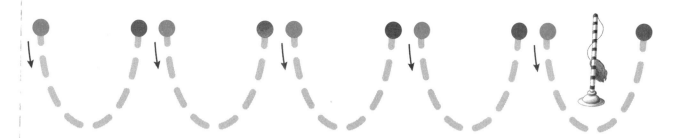

Sorting Letters

Timon and Pumbaa love to snack on wiggly grubs. Sometimes, the grubs make the shape of letters. Sort and write the letter shapes. The first one has been done for you.

M   Z   P   V

Q   O   S   C   N

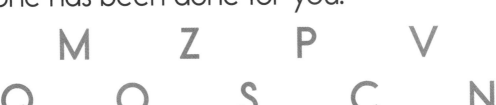

Curves	No Curves
) (	\ /
Q	M

Now sort and write these letters into the shapes.

The first one has been done for you.

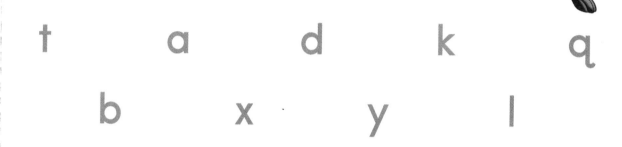

t   a   d   k   q

b   x   y   l

Letters with
Just Straight
Lines

t

Letters with
Balls and Lines

b

Sort and Match A to E

Donald, Huey, Dewey, and Louie spot lots of letters on the signs. Sort and write the letters shown below.

A B C D E

Letters with Straight Lines

Letters with Curves

Do some letters fit into both shapes?

Match the letters. The first one has been done for you.

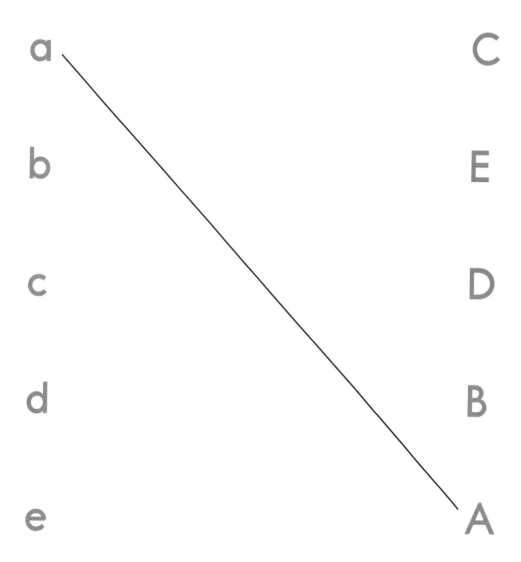

a   C

b   E

c   D

d   B

e   A

Learn Together

Help your child sort the letters. They might put the **B** or **D** in the box or the circle. Talk about the letters' features. ("The letter D has a curve **and** a straight line.") Challenge your child to add lowercase letters to the shapes.

Sort and Match F to J

Animals of all kinds live in the Pride Lands. You can find everything from flamingos to jackals. Sort and write the letters from F to j written below.

F g h I j

Lowercase Letters

Uppercase Letters

Fill in the missing uppercase or lowercase letter.

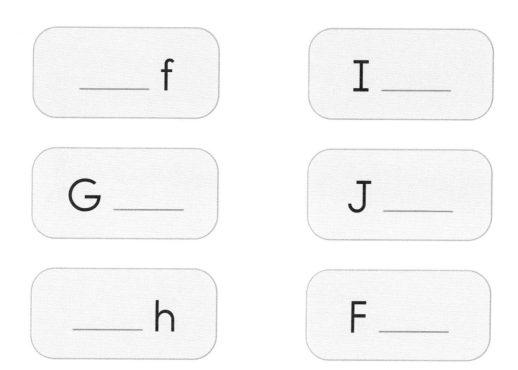

____ f

I ____

G ____

J ____

____ h

F ____

Aa Bb Cc Dd Ee Ff Gg Hh Ii Jj Kk
Ll Mm Nn Oo Pp Qq Rr Ss Tt Uu
Vv Ww Xx Yy Zz

Sort and Match K to O

Tiana is a great cook in the kitchen...especially with onions! Sort and write the letters from k to o written below.

k l m n o

Letters with Humps

Letters without Humps

Match the letters.
The first one has been done for you.

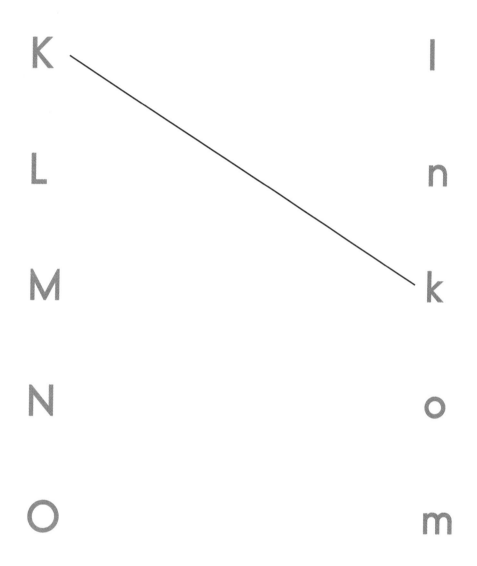

Sort and Match P to T

Mickey loves playing in the trees. Sort and write the letters from P to T written below.

P   Q   R   S   T

Letters with Holes

Letters without Holes

Fill in the missing uppercase or lowercase letter.

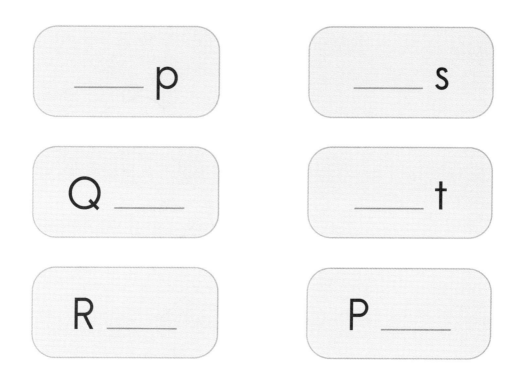

_____ p

_____ s

Q _____

_____ t

R _____

P _____

Aa Bb Cc Dd Ee Ff Gg Hh Ii Jj Kk
Ll Mm Nn Oo Pp Qq Rr Ss Tt Uu
Vv Ww Xx Yy Zz

Learn Together

Talk about how the uppercase and lowercase letters are similar and different. Which letter has a hole in its uppercase form but no hole in its lowercase form? (**Rr**)

Learning Letters

Connect the letters of the alphabet in order to finish the picture of Cinderella. Color the picture when you have connected all of the dots.

Find and circle all of the hidden letters in the picture below.

Let's Count!

Bugs are all over the jungle.

Count the ladybugs.

 = |

Count the beetles.

 = 2

Count the beetles.

= 3

24

Count the butterflies.

 = 4

Count the beetles.

 = 5

Count the ladybugs.

 = 6

Count the butterflies.

 = 7

Learn Together

With your child, collect 5 small objects (crayons, beads, toy cars). Take turns asking for different numbers of objects, up to 5.

How Many?

Daisy and Goofy
visit the stable.

Daisy feeds the horses.
Count the pails.

= 6

Goofy brushes the horses.
Count the brushes.

= 7

Count the ribbons.

 = 8

Count the hats.

= 9

Count the coats.

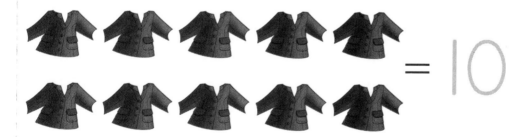 = 10

One to One

Merida loves to practice archery and make treats.

Match each number to the correct group. The first one is done for you.

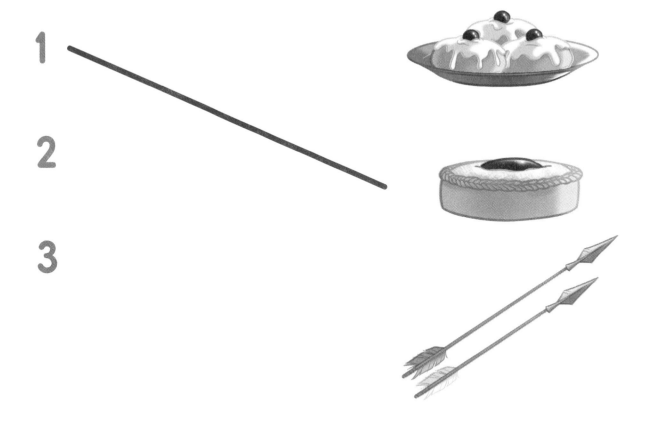

1

2

3

Merida bakes **1** pie.
Draw **1** pie.

Merida gives her friends **2** cakes.
Draw **2** cakes.

Merida shoots **3** arrows during practice.
Draw **3** arrows.

One to One

Mickey and Minnie host a talent show.

Match each number to the correct group. The first one is done for you.

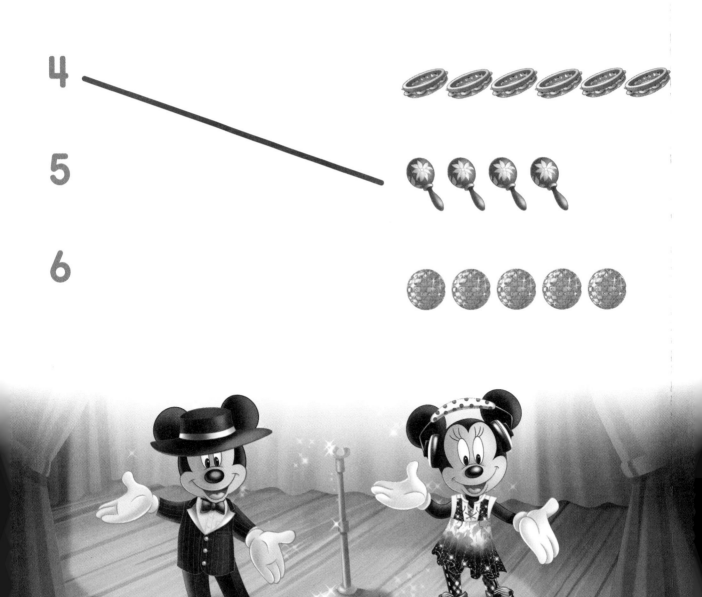

4

5

6

Minnie sings 4 songs.
Draw 4 music notes.

Mickey sings 5 songs.
Draw 5 music notes.

Daisy sings 6 songs.
Draw 6 music notes.

Learn Together

Place 6 pieces of paper labeled 1 to 6 in the 6 segments of a muffin tin.
Ask your child to put the correct number of objects (buttons, paper clips)
in each segment. With your child, count the objects as they go in.

One to One

You can find lots of footprints in the jungle.

Match each number to the correct group.
The first one is done for you.

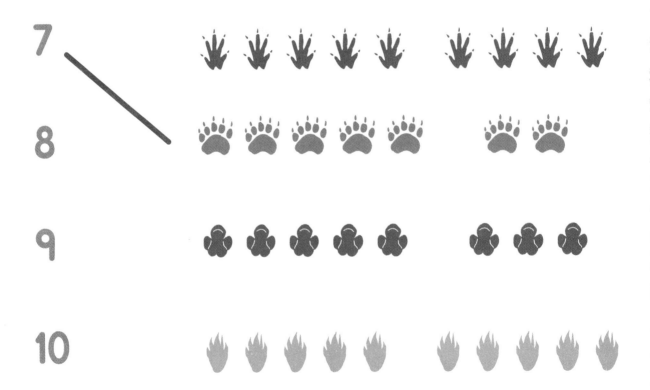

7

8

9

10

A path contains footprints from two different animals.

How many of each print was on the path? Match each number to the correct number of prints. The first one is done for you.

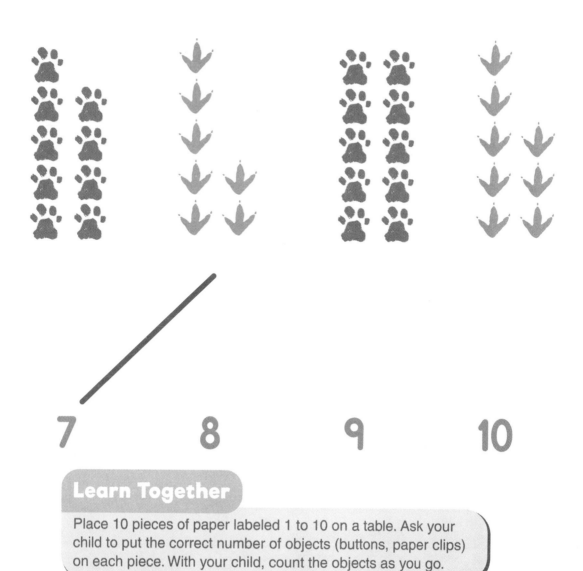

7   8   9   10

Enchanting Patterns

(Circle) the object
that comes next.

Circle the object that comes next.

Learn Together

Look for patterns in your home. Even the way you set the table can be a pattern for your child to identify: fork, plate, cup, fork, plate, cup.

Patterns in Nature

Patterns repeat over and over. Let's explore patterns made with leaves.

(Circle) the leaf in the box that comes next.

Circle the leaf in the box that comes next.

Circle the leaf in the box that comes next.

Making Patterns

Minnie sees patterns
in her garden.

Color the flowers
to complete
each pattern.

Goofy and Mickey see patterns at the park.

Make a pattern with the butterflies. Use 2 colors.

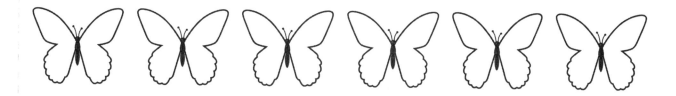

Make a pattern with the kites. Use 2 colors.

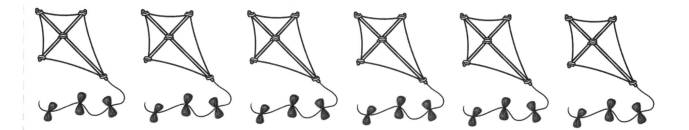

Learn Together

Help your child make patterns with buttons. Show your child how to make patterns that go up or down on a page, or from left to right on a page.

Which One Is Taller?

Mulan looks at the items around her to find the taller ones.

(Circle) the candle that is taller.

(Circle) the branch that is taller.

(Circle) the lantern that is the tallest.

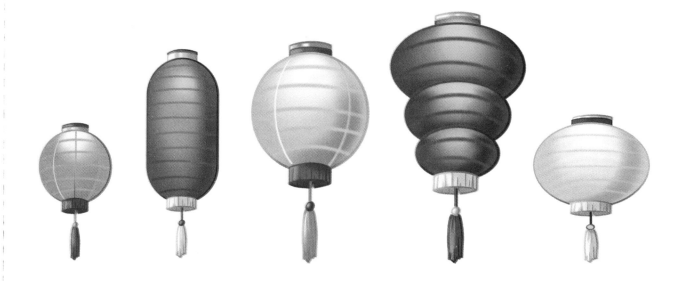

Which Is Shorter?

Daisy tosses cans into the recycling bin.

Circle the recycling bin that is shorter.

(Circle) the object
in each group
that is shorter.

Which One Is Bigger?

These special shapes from the Pride Lands come in different sizes.

The shape on the left is bigger than the shape on the right.

(Circle) the symbol that is bigger.

(Circle) the symbol that is bigger.

44

Draw a round symbol that is bigger than the one below.

Draw a square symbol that is bigger than the one below.

Which One Is Smaller?

The bowl is smaller than Figaro.

(Circle) the cat toy that is smaller.

(Circle) the ribbon that is smaller.

Preschool Basic Skills © Disney CD-705390

Draw a circle that is smaller than the one below.

Draw a triangle that is smaller than the one below.

Squares

The chess board has shapes that look like squares.

This is a square.

A square has 4 sides.

Trace the square.

Rectangles

Rugs in the palace have shapes that look like rectangles.

This is a rectangle.

A rectangle has 4 sides.
2 sides are long.
2 sides are short.

Trace the rectangle.

Triangles

Hyena teeth are shaped like triangles.

This is a triangle.

A triangle has 3 sides.

Trace the triangle.

Circles

The moon is shaped like a circle.

This is a circle.

A circle is round.

Trace the circle.

Ovals

Daisy walks past an **oval** mirror.

This is an **oval**.

An **oval** is shaped like a circle that is stretched out.

Trace the **oval**.

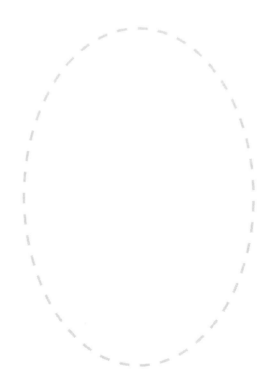

Shapes!

The brothers love
to paint shapes.

Draw a friend
for this robot
using lots of shapes.

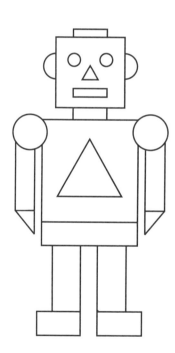

Learn Together

On paper, draw shapes (circle, square, rectangle).
Ask your child to color each shape a different color.
Ask them the name of each shape.

Shapes!

Rapunzel uses all kinds of shapes in her art. Color the shapes.

Color the **squares** red.

Color the **circles** blue.

Color the **rectangles** yellow.

Color the shapes.

Color the rectangles yellow.

Color the triangles orange.

Color the ovals green.

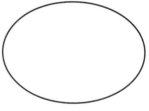
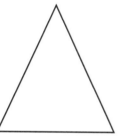

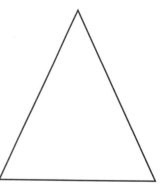
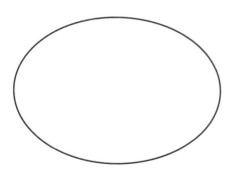

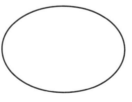

Learn Together

With your child, use a piece of string 12 inches (30 centimeters) long to create a shape. Take turns creating the shapes on this page.

Congratulations

to

_____

for completing this workbook!

Keep up the good work!

Color the pictures. Great job!

What Is Your Name?

This is Mickey.
Mickey is his name.
Print your name.

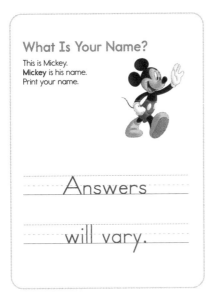

_____

Answers

will vary.

Draw a picture of yourself.

Drawings
will vary.

Learn Together
Help your child print their name, saying each
letter as you print it. With your child, sound out
their name. Point to and say each letter.

4   **5**

Sorting Letters

Timon and Pumbaa love
to snack on wiggly grubs.
Sometimes, the grubs make
the shape of letters. Sort and
write the letter shapes. The
first one has been done for you.

M   Z   P   V
Q   O   S   C   N

Curves	No Curves
⊃ ⊂	∨
Q	**M**
O	Z
S	V
P	N
C	

Now sort and write these letters
into the shapes.

The first one has been done for you.

t   a   d   k   q
b   x   y   l

Letters with Just Straight Lines	Letters with Balls and Lines
t	b
	a d
x k y l	q

Learn Together
Say each letter as you and your child sort,
describing its characteristics. Talk about the shapes
of letters and what your child notices.

Sort and Match A to E

Donald, Huey, Dewey, and
Louie spot lots of letters on
the signs. Sort and write the
letters shown below.

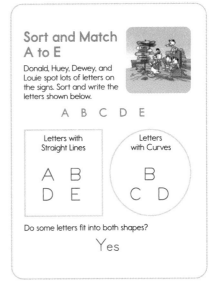

A B C D E

Letters with Straight Lines	Letters with Curves
A B	B
D E	C D

Do some letters fit into both shapes?

Yes

12   **13**   **14**

Match the letters. The first one has been done for you.

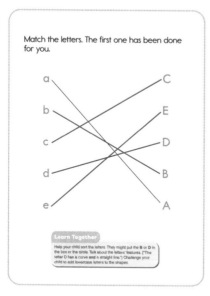

a   C
b   E
c   D
d   B
e   A

Learn Together
Help your child sort the letters. They might put the B or D in the box or the circle. Talk about the letters' features. ("The letter D has a curve and a straight line.") Challenge your child to add lowercase letters to the shapes.

15

Sort and Match F to J

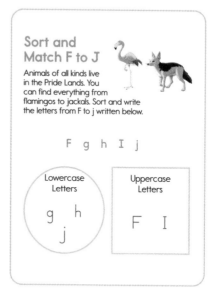

Animals of all kinds live in the Pride Lands. You can find everything from flamingos to jackals. Sort and write the letters from F to j written below.

F   g   h   I   j

Lowercase Letters

g   h
j

Uppercase Letters

F   I

16

Fill in the missing uppercase or lowercase letter.

F f   I i
G g   J j
H h   F f

Aa Bb Cc Dd Ee Ff Gg Hh Ii Jj Kk
Ll Mm Nn Oo Pp Qq Rr Ss Tt Uu
Vv Ww Xx Yy Zz

Learn Together
Help your child compare the features of the uppercase and lowercase letters. Encourage your child to describe the movement of their pencil as they write each letter.

17

Sort and Match K to O

Tiana is a great cook in the kitchen...especially with onions! Sort and write the letters from k to o written below.

k   l   m   n   o

Letters with Humps

m   n
o

Letters without Humps

k   l

18

Match the letters. The first one has been done for you.

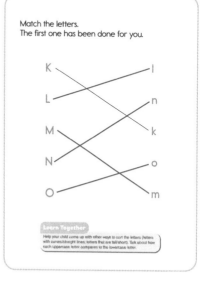

K   l
L   n
M   k
N   o
O   m

Learn Together
Help your child come up with other ways to sort the letters (letters with curves/straight lines; letters that are tall/short). Talk about how each uppercase letter compares to the lowercase letter.

19

Sort and Match P to T

Mickey loves playing in the trees. Sort and write the letters from P to T written below.

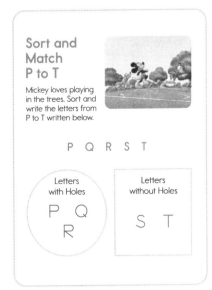

P Q R S T

Letters with Holes

P Q R

Letters without Holes

S T

20

Fill in the missing uppercase or lowercase letter.

P p   S s

Q q   T t

R r   P p

Aa Bb Cc Dd Ee Ff Gg Hh Ii Jj Kk
Ll Mm Nn Oo Pp Qq Rr Ss Tt Uu
Vv Ww Xx Yy Zz

Learn Together

Talk about how the uppercase and lowercase letters are similar and different. Which letter has a hole in its uppercase form but no hole in its lowercase form? (Rr)

21

Learning Letters

Connect the letters of the alphabet in order to finish the picture of Cinderella. Color the picture when you have connected all of the dots.

22

Find and circle all of the hidden letters in the picture below.

23

One to One

Merida loves to practice archery and make treats.

Match each number to the correct group. The first one is done for you.

1
2
3

28

Merida bakes 1 pie.
Draw 1 pie.

Drawings will vary.

Merida gives her friends 2 cakes.
Draw 2 cakes.

Merida shoots 3 arrows during practice.
Draw 3 arrows.

29

One to One

Mickey and Minnie host a talent show.

Match each number to the correct group. The first one is done for you.

4
5
6

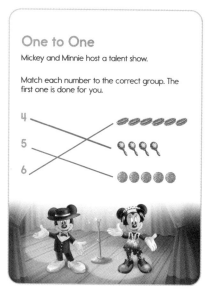

30

Minnie sings 4 songs.
Draw 4 music notes.

Mickey sings 5 songs.
Draw 5 music notes.

Daisy sings 6 songs.
Draw 6 music notes.

31

One to One

You can find lots of footprints in the jungle.

Match each number to the correct group.
The first one is done for you.

7
8
9
10

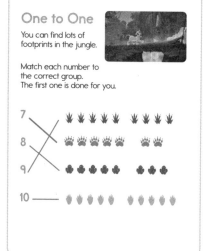

32

A path contains footprints from two different animals.

How many of each print was on the path? Match each number to the correct number of prints. The first one is done for you.

7   8   9   10

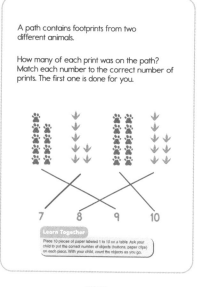

33

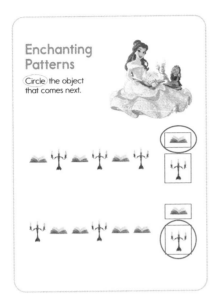

34

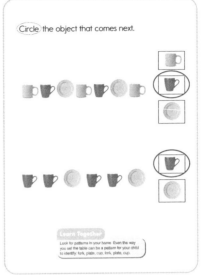

35

36

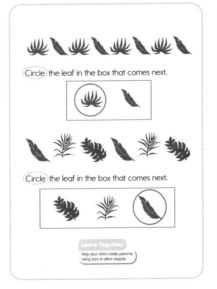

37

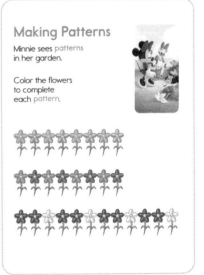

38

Goofy and Mickey see patterns at the park.

Make a pattern with the butterflies. Use 2 colors.

Make a pattern with the kites. Use 2 colors.

Patterns will vary.

Learn Together
Help your child make patterns with buttons. Show your child how to make patterns that go up or down on a page, or from left to right on a page.

39

Which One Is Taller?

Mulan looks at the items around her to find the taller ones.

Circle the candle that is taller.

Circle the branch that is taller.

40

Circle the lantern that is the tallest.

41

Which Is Shorter?

Daisy tosses cans into the recycling bin.

Circle the recycling bin that is shorter.

42

Circle the object in each group that is shorter.

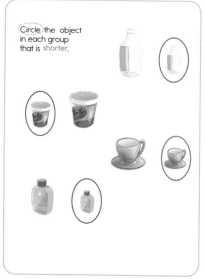

43

Which One Is Bigger?

These special shapes from the Pride Lands come in different sizes.
The shape on the left is bigger than the shape on the right.

Circle the symbol that is bigger.

Circle the symbol that is bigger.

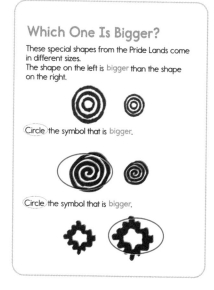

44

Draw a round symbol that is bigger than the one below.

Drawings will vary.

Draw a square symbol that is bigger than the one below.

Drawings will vary.

Learn Together
With your child, compare the sizes of objects around your home. Encourage your child to use the word bigger.

45

Which One Is Smaller?

The bowl is smaller than Figaro.

Circle the cat toy that is smaller.

Circle the ribbon that is smaller.

46

Draw a circle that is smaller than the one below.

Drawings will vary.

Draw a triangle that is smaller than the one below.

Drawings will vary.

Learn Together
With your child, compare the sizes of objects around your home. Encourage your child to use the word smaller.

47

Shapes!

The brothers love to paint shapes.

Draw a friend for this robot using lots of shapes.

Drawings will vary.

Learn Together
On paper, draw shapes (circle, square, rectangle). Ask your child to color each shape a different color. Ask them the name of each shape.

53

Shapes!

Rapunzel uses all kinds of shapes in her art. Color the shapes.

Color the squares red.

Color the circles blue.

Color the rectangles yellow.

54

Color the shapes.

Color the rectangles yellow.

Color the triangles orange.

Color the ovals green.

Learn Together
With your child, use a piece of string 12 inches (30 centimeters) long to create a shape. Take turns creating the shapes on this page.

55